978-1-7377808-4-7
Copyright @ 2023 Laura Bandy
Published by Gold Wake Press
Cover Design by Kevin Stone
Book Interior by Paul Brooke
No part of this book may be reproduced
except in brief quotations and reviews
without permission from the publisher.
Monster Movie published 2023.
goldwake.com

Monster Movie

Acknowledgements

The author would like to thank and acknowledge the publications where these poems first appeared: *Alluvian,* "Weathervane," September 2022; Barrelhouse Blog, "Downstate," (new title "Monster Movie,") October 2017; *Coffin Bell,* "My AI," October 2021; *The Cossack Review,* "Why I Love the Prose Poem," (new title "The Girl Detective") April 2015; *Dreich Magazine,* "Ode to the Dancing Girls," and "The End is the Beginning" Driftwood Press; "I'm worst at what I do best," January 2022; *Fatal Flaw,* "The 400 Blows," November 2020; *The Florida Review,* "Dumb Bitch," January 2022; *The Laurel Review,* "Charley Horse," June 2020; *Longleaf Review,* "Corsage," May 2021; *Midwest Review,* "Interregnum" and "Actionville," July 2020; *Moist Poetry Journal,* "We've Hardly Begun And," December 2021; *NonBinary Review,* "Trick," March 2021; *Pine Row,* "Vodka and Houseplants," November 2020; *Pithead Chapel,* "Lunar Eclipse," December 2017; *River Styx,* "All-American Extraterrestrial" and "Choose Your Own Adventure," December 2017; Rondeau Roundup, Trio of Triolets Contest, 1st Prize: "Tom Petty's American Girl," "Triolet 007," and "Pick-up Line Triolet with Cocaine, Elbo Room," December 2017; *Trailer Park Quarterly,* "Ode to the Bramford," winter 2017; *Triggerfish Critical Review,* "Cinema," "Hack," and "Tech Enters the Midwest," December 2017; *TYPO,* "Baby Shower Torture Porn," March 2019

And thanks to Tarl, my love; Sarah Alice, my other self; and Michael Van Walleghen, best poet and teacher—how I wish you were here.

TABLE OF CONTENTS

I. Previews

Locusts I: Summer, 1987   11
The Girl Detective   12
Road Trip Picture   13
Coming of Age Flick: Pink Cupcakes   14
Word Problems: I. Asynchronous Learning   15
                II. Downhill   16
After the Proposal   17
Fellini's Trick   18
Lunar Eclipse   19
Home Movie   20
Ode to the Dancing Girls, Escape from New York   21
Slasher: Run   22
I'm worse at what I do best   23
Vodka and Houseplants   24
Weathervane   25
Figure Model: Drawing 101   26
Ode to Shooter   28
The 400 Blows   29
Jailhouse Rock   30
Thigh Gap   31
Cinema   33
Ode to the Bramford, Rosemary's Baby   34
Election Night Noir: Chicago, 2000   35
Early Aught's Drama: Hansen's Basement, Wicker Park   36
Pick-up Line Triolet with Cocaine: Elbo Room   38
Alan Solomon's Gold Coast   39
The End is the Beginning   40
South Side Sonnet   41
Triolet 007: My Biopic   42
Locusts II: Winter, 2006   43

II.   **Feature**

Haunted House II: The Return   45
Interregnum   46
Ceci n'est pas une pipe   47
Baby Shower Torture Porn   48
Bad Robot   49
Ode to the Rain, Three Days of the Condor   50
Fat Tuesday in New Orleans   51
Short Film   52
Corsage   53
Actionville   54
All American Extraterrestrial   55
Movie Soundtrack: Tom Petty's "American Girl"   56
Period Piece   57
Body Horror: Biopsy   58
Ode to the Barn Raising Scene, Peter Weir's Witness   59
In a Capsule of the Tanning Salon   60
John Hughes Redux   61
Slapstick: Ear Re-Piercing with Attendant Lexi at Claire's Boutique   62
Tech Enters the Midwest   63
Choose Your Own Adventure   64
Charley Horse   65
Rated R: Dumb Bitch   66
Graffiti Rondeau   67
Ode to "Sikiliza Kwa Wahenga," Get Out   68
Rerun   69
We've Hardly Begun And   71
Ode to Lynyrd Skynyrd, "Tuesday's Gone"   72
Monster Movie   73

III.   **Credits**

Hate Watch   75

IV.   **Post-Credits**

Faithful   77

"Who are you? What are you? Where did you come from? I think you're the cause of all this…"
—The Birds

Locusts I. Summer, 1987

They covered everything. I was small.
I watched my father through the kitchen window, wrestling
a garden hose come alive, entangling his legs.
The stream washed the insects from the trees.

They lifted from the grass, clouded around my father
who dropped to the ground and rolled away like a man on fire.
Then they reached the house, winging against aluminum siding,
the window where I stood. Their eyes were the red of altar wine

I wasn't allowed to drink, and gold-green wings reminded me
of my pastor's embroidered robes. Sometimes
the way he talked about heaven made me want to die—just for a while,
just to see it. Lifting arms high Sunday mornings, his voice echoed

against stone walls, and his hands unfolded over the congregation. The sun
blazed through stained glass, and when I closed my eyes, I was somewhere
else, a princess land where I ruled kindly over all… If I dozed off, slumping
on my side, mother covered me, tugged down the bottom of my skirt—

I couldn't see my father anymore. He was somewhere beyond
the window's frame and insects were swarming up the glass.
Where was mother? I wanted to help, turned the crank
that spread the heavy pane outward like someone blowing a kiss.

A scorched breeze alive with humming bodies
blew past. I tried to pull the window shut again, but the handle
wouldn't budge. A few caught in my hair, stuck against my damp neck,
and when I opened my mouth to scream, they crawled inside.

The Girl Detective

The freezer was at the bottom of the cellar stairs. When I was young, I would go down there in summer and shake from the cold blast, heat rushing behind me, frost-numbed and feverish all at once until I couldn't take it—grabbed for lime ices, bomb pops, root beer slush. There were two plastic baggies in the back behind an ancient rump roast. One held an Indigo Bunting. The other held a Scarlet Tanager. Fact: my mother was a birder. Fact: we had a large picture window and sometimes birds mistook it for sky. In my spare time, I read encyclopedias which were locked in my father's study. I had a key, like Nancy Drew. I wanted to learn something that was true, solve the case of the silent house. Fact: Indigo Buntings are indigenous to Southern Canada, "a brilliantly blue bird of old fields and roadsides." Fact: Scarlet Tanagers are natives of the eastern interior and, "despite vivid coloring might be overlooked because of rather secretive behavior." Sometimes I would remove the birds from their clear casings and climb back up the cellar steps into the yard with one in each hand. Mid-August, the wind would whip over our scorched cornfields and blow the weathervane in circles so fast it blurred, becoming every direction.

Road Trip Picture

After my mother made coffee with the gasoline funnel and the grownups started vomiting, and after my brother got lost in the Badlands for hours, everyone fearing the worst, I slammed the car door shut on my twin's hand, and the tornado hit Salina. I can't recall her screams: "Like someone being stabbed" my father marveled later, but I remember knowing we had to take cover. Crouched under a ping pong table in the hotel basement, water seeping down the walls from the storm outside, I thought about stories from church camp. If we were being tested, parents still green from the gasoline, brother silent since his wanderings in the desert, and sister moaning for more pills with broken fingers swaddled in her lap, then I alone had been spared. Was this what it meant to be chosen?

When they discovered her pain medicine was still in the car, I volunteered and no one stopped me from walking out into the night, sky a color I'd never seen, the yellow I'd imagined my sister's skin when she almost died at our birth, I healthy in the next crib and delivered to this moment in a far-off land. The rain lashed down, and across the parking lot, across wheat fields that stretched for miles, I saw the heavens tear, spit out a loop of wind that spun just for me, like a snake that rises, writhing, and I knew this story too, understood the consequences of knowledge so that I wanted to be lifted, taken away from this place and the broken people in the basement who were clearly marked for death, away from this vacation in too-small rooms, I could hear my mother's nightly pleas—"Let's end this, please, how much worse will we allow it to get"—I kept my eyes wide open as the funnel spun closer because to witness was what I was born for.

Coming of Age Flick: Pink Cupcakes

In eighth grade, I went to a birthday party at Amy O'Neal's house. She was almost popular, although the right girls hadn't shown up and the tension made her voice weak. "Okay, cupcakes!" she squeaked, herding us into her bedroom which was really a closet. There were no streamers or balloons, and we ate on the bed. I tried not to spill, watching her mother through the swinging beads, cigarette between her lips as she stirred a pitcher of red Kool-Aid. The house was hidden at the end of a street I'd never seen. From far away, it seemed impressive: white, three stories, with tall columns and a balcony. Closer up, you could see the seams, the rotting beams and sagging underneath. The house was sinking. "Let's go up on the terrace," I suggested with a sweep of my arm, but Amy said the stairs were tricky and they only rented the bottom floor anyway. "We could explore the neighborhood," she said, studying her nail polish, "Robby Sims lives a few houses over." We moved together through the front door onto a dark block, every streetlamp dim or broken, our whispers tangling in the night air. Someone had made a paper fortune teller, and we passed it around as we walked. I would marry a poor man and live in a beach hut with beautiful babies, not the future I was hoping for. At the train tracks, I placed pebbles on the rails then myself, flexing wrists against imagined ropes and crying, "Oh Robby, save me, save me!" Amy scowled; said we should get back before her mother left for her boyfriend's place. "Sometimes he stays over," she said, "I've seen them together. She lets him put his face down there." I felt strange when she spoke, as though someone was lifting my own skirt. "Do you know what that's called?" she asked me confidently, in charge of her party now, and I did, and I said it although the words felt wrong in my mouth; the abode of my body blown open for all to see. We heard the sirens then and caught a faint hint of smoke curling in the late summer air, fragrant with tall grass and sweet alyssum. "Someone's house is on fire," Amy said, looking back the way we came. The next day, when it was much too late, the firemen would speculate about young girls and curling irons, candles, open flame.

Word Problems

I.   Asynchronous Learning

I sat in Algebra and thought about boys. Like magic, they appeared
outside the classroom window. Ms. Goss droned on with her impossible

equations while I watched two rugby-shirted blondes pass briskly
just beneath the glass. No one else seemed to note their progress,

all heads bent studiously to hieroglyphic sums. Some thought it strange
that our school sat surrounded on all sides by corn, but I liked

the swaying stalks, tall and tightly aligned in spring, a bright green
army. I noticed the boys were dragging something between them,

spied a shock of dyed blue mohawk and Misfits-stickered skateboard
that bespoke sophomore thrasher Jake Tosh, and when his head snapped

side-angle, I saw his zero of a mouth shouting something solved
into silence as the planted rows swallowed them all. Here was math

I could follow: two boys clad head to toe in Polo + one trailer park punk
whose dad had inexplicably gone to Harvard = a beating in the fields.

How dare he? How dare any of us, I mused, scanning the room for an ally
who might take the hit instead of me. When no one met my eye, I began

to raise my hand half-heartedly to tell, felt a sharp kick to my shin. Susan,
the cheerleader assigned a seat beside me, who liked Hallmark cards, gin

and tonics, and her sleepy quarterback boyfriend, was displeased. "He
was asking for it," she whispered, then passed me a Luden's cherry cough drop

in solidarity. *Well, I tried,* I thought, placed the sweet spoils on my tongue
and wondered what it felt like to be punched. Outside, late afternoon sun

bled fading orange over tall corn inviolate and solid, a wall impassable
even if someone wanted. "Pay attention," Ms. Goss said then, "or you'll fail this class."

II.   Downhill

On our Christian ski trip in a sad Wisconsin town, Chad Rader stood at the lip
of a vertiginous drop, waved shyly, then vanished from view, down the Black Diamond

backwards. I often watched his circles around our high school track in gym, running
in a way I'd never seen a human run before, like his body was created for just this sum—

sunny day + long legs = twenty perfect laps. His race was middle distance and, as track manager,
I had seen him take the 3000 meter in eight minutes flat, a record at state. But backwards

down a mountain balanced precariously on cheap rental skis? What kind of animal was he,
and could I be of the same sleek species? It was more than speed, it was beauty, too—

an ineffable grace that marked him, surely, as chosen. We were learning so much on this trip
about God and his plans for us, how he would give with both hands if we only agreed

to meet him halfway. For us girls, this meant covering arms to the hands and legs to the calf,
carrying our Bibles everywhere, even class, and praying to be more like Mary, Mother of God

so as to avoid hell. For boys, rules seemed looser— no dress code required and larger cast of characters
to copy; like stern, waters-parting Moses, and Paul, who got to be naughty then good once scales fell.

When I accidentally opened the door to the wrong room on our trip's second night,
reproachful chaperones shook their heads and sent me away; men guarding boys

all bent to the ground and crying, "I repent, I repent!" And later that same night, lost
on my quest for ice, I opened a wrong door once more to find Chad and Missy Brady

intertwined, only pausing their unclad clutch to whisper-scream that I leave. One more makes three,
I thought, feeling very Jesus-y and beleaguered to be shut out twice, as though Peter himself

had betrayed me. Would I never know sin wicked enough to bring me to my knees, or grow
physical attributes so ample that handsome track stars would seek me out in the dark? I knew

those thoughts were not appropriate for virtuous women, but I had them anyway, stewing
over Bible verse flashcards in my hotel room while roommates snored in blameless sleep.

That long night was the beginning of the breach, a falling away, eventually, from my faith.
But demands of the story follow me, and though the good book says no prophecy ever arose

by will of man, still there were those who spoke from God when moved by the Holy Spirit. Whatever
speaks through me today, be it celestial or more earthly, I look back to tell trip guardians of our purity

that they were too late, and what possible business was it of theirs, anyway? I say to Missy Brady,
reconsider the move to Florida and aerobics studio purchase, you will regret both come 2020. And

with my final prophecy twenty years too late, twenty laps around the sun, I speak to Chad directly—
forsake your sacred motorcycle. Who wouldn't long to feel the wind blow past the way it did in youth?

You can never return to the track. A hard truth, heaven knows, but heed me—delay the wreck
and coma. Take a longer backwards way and savor that last downhill run, the final door to close.

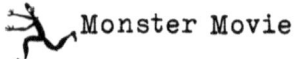

After the Proposal

My turn to ride the tractor, I drove it into the side of a barn. It was decided I was a passenger from that point on. Kim dug a snow disc out of the cellar along with a length of rope she hooked onto the back of the tractor. I sat folded up like a pocketknife, admiring the lines of my knees. We were studying figures in Geometry, and I discovered that my bent limbs formed an obtuse angle inside the pink plastic circle. This senior year was the first I'd ever been good at math, and suddenly the world seemed all dots and edges. My body held so many shapes within—tubes, rooms, womb. "Hold on," Kim said, handing me the knotted end of rope and sputtering the tractor to life. She drove slow loops around the yard, waving at the yellow squares of window on our farmhand's trailer and getting lapped by his toy poodle, Goliath. The sky was streaked pink, and a sinking sun shot final rays over cornfields in the distance, connecting each row like a child's coloring book. "They would give you the farm," Kim said over her shoulder, taking a sharp turn at the fence line. "You know there's no one else to work it." I could feel new grass beneath me and hidden rocks and twigs as I slid in a shifting V behind the tractor, my disc spinning like a star that can't find its place in the constellation.

Fellini's Trick

I didn't remember walking to school, but there I was, waiting for the eclipse. I watched anxiously out the classroom window, but the sun looked like it always looked. Or was it redder? Blonder? On the cartoons, they had promised an early afternoon eclipse, perfect timing to get out of my math quiz. This was art, which I didn't mind. My teacher held up a pinhole box camera, two thin white pieces of cardboard fastened side by side with a tiny hole in the middle. "Every massive particle in the universe attracts every other massive particle with a force that is directly proportional to the product of their masses and inversely proportional to the square of the distance between them," she said to the class. "Now you try." On the desk in front of me: scissors, cardboard, black paint, a top hat, scotch tape and a needle. My hands were sweaty. I hated math. I cobbled a small box together and smeared paint inside, so it was light proof. It was growing darker in the room and everyone else seemed to be finished, picking up their cameras and following our teacher out of the water. "This part's sticky," said Tom, sitting behind me. Tom was sitting beside me. I had loved him for a long time. He was so red and blonde. "Here, I'll keep it still," he said, and held the rabbit in front of me. "Push it straight through or you won't be able to see the eclipse." I had the needle in my hand. The black X I had painted on his fur still marked the spot. There was hardly any mess. "Now go outside and stare at the sun," said Tom the rabbit. "Keep looking until we see the whites of your eyes, that's the trick."

Lunar Eclipse

A secret trail through neighbor's backyards led to Ginny's house
blue light from our television flickering farther and farther behind.
Ginny was out front, dragging a stick through overgrown grass. "Look,"
she said, "the moon is covered in blood." She was always
saying things, but the moon was a strange color— dark scarlet,
swollen like a tick. We took turns at a rotten slit in the fence
spying on the Ankrom twins coaxing a girl to show them
something. Their parents were never home. Moonlit,
her bare skin seemed to smolder. "Sometimes they come over,"
Ginny said, "those boys are wild." We watched for awhile
then backed away, went inside for dinner. The house
was dark, only glow a dim glimmer from the kitchen.
Her parents were deaf, and the phone was hooked up
to a yellow lightbulb. It would flash suddenly and the walls
would shudder. "I'm cooking tonight," Ginny said, "they
teach late. Here," and she handed me a long knife.
There was a frozen chicken on the counter, but I didn't know
what to do with it. Experimenting, I slid my knife into the hole
beneath, twisted until bloody pieces trailed out. "I'll do it,"
Ginny said, plunged her hand in and pulled out the rest.
She was good at everything, and I was a fast learner. Maybe we
would cast spells later, be remade as witches in the carmine night.
There was a scratching at the back-screen door that ceased
my reverie. "Either Apollo got out or it's the boys," Ginny said,
pulled a chain-link dog leash from the wall. "Let's go see."

Home Movie

Ginny made dinner while we waited for her parents to get home. They taught night classes at the school for the deaf, so I would walk home with her after school and play Atari, watch movies, read books in their absence. Ginny was the only friend who liked to read as much as me. This week, it was *The Westing Game* and Nancy Drew mysteries. Sometimes the movies we watched were scary. I wasn't allowed to see *First Born* at home, but I wasn't home. In the movie, the stepfather turned out to be dangerous, violent. The oldest son had to protect the younger one from something bad happening. Ginny signed the whole time without realizing it; she did that a lot. Through the window, I watched the sun go down and fireflies rise. It was strange to realize that they were glowing the same outside my home, so close by. Shouldn't time stop there when I was away? Ginny's house reminded me of my own. The sense of something hidden. When her parents arrived, I took the meatloaf out of the oven and filled glasses with Tang while Ginny signed to her parents, speaking along with the signs. Why couldn't they ever make it home on time? Who cared about the debate team? They always lost anyway, and the meatloaf would be dry. When we finally sat down to dinner, there was silence while Mr. Myers carved listlessly at the shriveled main dish, and then Ginny lifted a glass to her lips and screamed and screamed.

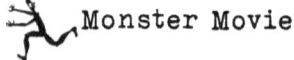

Ode to the Dancing Girls, John Carpenter's Escape from New York

The girls are boys of course, dolled up in dirty frocks and dancing with abandon on the bombed-out Met stage. NYC is maximum security now, the prison women gone almost entirely into hiding, while the men dress in drag and perform their show. In Marie Antoinette wigs, they offer high kicks and heartfelt lyrics for Snake Plissken, fresh meat inmate late of bank robberies and Leningrad battles, he stumbles into their performance with explosives set to blow in his arteries if the mission goes bent. It's a whole thing involving the U.S. President and a group of semi-humans called the Crazies who live in subway tunnels and enjoy torture more than most, so those dancing girls are the last sweet sight Snake will have for some time, pink and yellow crinolines flaring in hot lights as they twirl like pinwheels at a birthday party, like children who sneak cake and giddily spin past burnt out candles into the coming dark—*This is bliss, it's a lark, everyone's dying for New York!*

Slasher: Run
Jacksonville, Illinois Kiwanis Haunted House, 1991

The man in the Jason mask puts down his chainsaw
picks up tiny Kelly, and carries her away

screaming. We're at the haunted house
in our small town, every room a run

of recent horror: *Children of the Corn,
Friday the 13th, Halloween.* It seems

Kiwanis has gone all out this year, blood
running the walls and floors, doors flung

wide to show, surprise! Another ghost.
All these corpses come from somewhere—

killer clowns bussed in from nearby Woodson,
White Hall, towns even smaller than ours

but flush in bodies eager to sow fear
for a cause—to chase with icepicks and knives

shuddering pre-teens so that they learn early
who the monsters are. The man who takes Kelly

is her father who has left her mother and misses
his kids. "Something he should have thought of

before he run out," says Kelly days later and matter of fact
while we walk by the Mobil factory at dusk, lot full

of second shift then over the tracks and past Capitol
bricks humming with the press of records, finally fields

of corn rustling as we lose the sun—"This is where the girl
in the movie usually dies," says Kelly. *Run.*

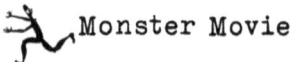

I'm worst at what I do best—*"Smells Like Teen Spirit" debuts on MTV, September 10, 1991*

Ray hands me a beer. He's cheating on me
with my best friend, but I don't know it yet. Ray is my first
love. Mick is Ray's best friend. Mick is in love with me
but I don't know it yet. The Coors can is warm

and I think how beer doesn't taste very good. That will change
but I don't know it yet. Ray's mother in bed upstairs with satin sleeping mask
and "Sounds of the Beach" on repeat. I will date Ray for two years and never
meet her, but I don't know it yet. Ray is wearing a child's Hawaiian shirt

that half covers his frame. He is the first of three men over 6'5" that I'll date, all just
taller than my father, but I don't know it yet. His father left money on the table
for pizza before leaving. He's got a tumor in his gut like a sailor's knot
but we don't know it yet. Ray loves boats. When his father dies

in six months, Ray will row his father's boat out to the middle of Lime Lake
and sink it, almost sink himself, but we don't know it yet. Mick thinks
we should spend the money on nitrous. He buys oversized balloons to speak
in squeaks before really sucking it in. After inhaling eight balloons, I will stop breathing

for a minute, but we don't know it yet. Ray says the balloons make it a party
and we need noise, so he turns on the TV. Next week watching *Barney Miller*
and cleaning his gun, he will fall asleep, and his brother will load it. Ray will wake, not like
the episode, and shoot Wojciehowicz, but we don't know it yet. I want to watch *120 Minutes*

and the boys bump into each other reaching for the remote. I will sleep
with both of them before morning, but we don't know it yet. A music video
on screen from a band we've never seen, and Ray turns it up. The singer mumbles,
screams, and we're transfixed. Mick asks, "What's he saying?" but no one knows it yet.

Vodka and Houseplants: Urbana, Illinois 1998

The conflict in Chechnya is spilling into neighboring republics, escalating the process of destabilization.
    -Alexei Malashenko, Scholar-in-Residence, Carnegie Moscow Center

Denis Daneeka stands accused of robbing the till at the campus coffeehouse we tend, and I believe him innocent, believe the boss just doesn't like foreigners; he told me Slavs seem sneaky–"What are they hiding?" he wants to know. I invite Denis over for a drink. "Maybe some friends I bring along?" he asks, and I agree, eager to please. They all arrive together, and Denis roars in my doorway, "The tanks are rumbling through the streets!" He bows and hands me a potted orchid with the price tag still on that I carry in my arms most of the night. They don't seem to hear my offer of beers; Boris busy lowering the blinds, Val tuning the radio to a station I've never heard. "Black bread to start," says Galina, "vodka to finish." When I protest I have nothing to mix with the liquor, they laugh and ask politely for pickles. "All Americans have pickles," says Pasha. We drink vodka straight with brine chasers as the sun slides golden bars down my wall. Soon, we are all on the floor in a dark room. Boris keeps telling jokes without punch lines and he is toasted each time, "Za Vas! Za Vas!" A few double over with laughter as though they are actually in pain, and Denis whispers that these jokes are popular at home; that it's all in the telling, not the arrival. "Tell me about home," I say, moving closer so the smoke from my cigarette tangles like rope between us, "Tell me why you came here." Denis sighs, pinches my lit cigarette and smokes it down to the filter before burying the red end deep in orchid soil. He pats my cheek not unkindly. "We are not here," says Denis.

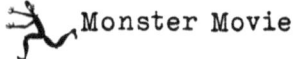

Weathervane

There are entire days when I forget
about the night, when in my blue Isuzu

I started down the drive to leave the party;
barely rolling, being careful on the gravel

car windows open, inviting in the heat
and grit of Midwest breeze in summer,

corn dust rising from the fields so that I choked
but found it sweet—fragrant prairie phlox

and milkweed twined with light late evening rain.
On the lawn, girls like blooms in bright orange

and blue, the colors of the school, still dancing
through the spate to Beck's "Loser," neon glow-sticks

spinning geometric traces in the air, while I eased
backwards, music and swaying lady flowers slowly

receding from view. I didn't want to leave, wanted
to remain in the bouquet sipping keg beer and unfurling

petals everywhere, but I was still good then and
a girl who is good knows when to leave my mother

taught me, or maybe it was the world who whispered be
nice again and again; *be nice,* so that when I paused

at the end of the driveway to look both ways and a boy
jumped lightly onto my running board, his ball cap backwards,

fraternity letters stitched large across his chest, I wanted to help.
He asked for a ride then pushed through my half open window

to say either I'm not going to hurt you or I'm going to hurt you,
I could not tell which. I felt the frost then that comes at summer's

end, the dusting of ice we wake to that bends the grass. Still, I laughed
and said sorry as he slid away. The next season had started—fall, with her

numbing cold and mess. Soon leaves would blaze artery red, console the loss.

Figure Model: Drawing 101

There are certain forensic truths we can know for sure. The rest of the story is made up of contested narratives.
                                    - NPR Program on Truth Commissions

You stand in a small room that has no ceiling, no handle
on the door. There is a hook, hang your clothes. The floor
is cold and stained with paint, black markings, messages.
Murmured voices through the wall reach you like dying stars.
Slide fingers into the sliver of light and step forward. Voices stop,
you remove your robe and then nothing covers you.

First there is a chair. Maybe the chair seems familiar, the one
they slid into a corner back in grade school, you stared
at the wall, or your father's armchair, he stared at nothing
or a chair with voltage, straps on the arms, you're here
for a reason. Sweat collects under your arms, purple bruise
on your thigh throbs— they don't want movement, pencils scrape.

Are you cold, do you need to stretch, this is the real thing now,
the long freeze. On your knees, drape the white sheet over stained
mattress two boys drag to the center of the room. How do they
want you? Laid low, eyes to ceiling, one arm reaching, left leg wrenched
beneath the right. Perhaps it all seems familiar, a scene from that play
set in a brothel, two sisters trapped together. At the end, one made it out

and the sister left behind sawed off her own leg. Your twin
enters. Of course, you can only see the top of her head, gaze
fixed high, but you know her, silent in the corner. She can't believe
you're here, what kind of person would share their body like this. Shift
and there's a hiss; "Her arm doesn't fall like that." They need stillness
these shadows surrounding; some standing, some crouched... Your twin

lowers her eyes, folds back one woolen sleeve to check the time, leaves
through a side door. It's just you in a room, immobile for hours marked
by a pool of sunlight stealing over the body beginning at bare toes, slowly
over ankles then legs exposed, black hairs peppered across white skin, final
slash of brilliance severs your thigh—"We could use some variation
in darkness," the instructor decides, drags down the blinds.

Ode to Shooter

Mark Wahlberg is Bobby Lee Swagger, and he loves his guns and his dog who gets killed in the first ten minutes of the film, all the shooting. Someone with a shotgun comes after Swagger then; it's military, it's personal, it is personally military, and the shooting continues, so much shooting! Bobby Lee meets a girl with kind eyes and a tourniquet, she applies pressure, cuts and pries bullets from Bobby who has been shot twice— one bullet, two bullet, red bullet, red. She heals him up with a winsome grin and leaky embrace, Romeo is still bleeding a little, shoot. But it's nice, their moment, and then he gets going, back to the shooting which waits for no man, especially the bad man who will enter when Bobby leaves, go on a tear to rape the pretty girl and shoot her, shoot her in the head, her long blonde hair fans in the blood and Bobby Lee gets ANGRY when he finds her, gets Blitzkrieg-y with a shooting spree so that bodies drop on top of each other to fill the streets like a death parade, body after body, dead after dead; with all that man meat, it's hard to tell the shooter from the shooted.

The 400 Blows

After my ex shoves me around a little, they get him out of there
and the green-jacket guy brings me a drink. "Are you okay?
                          Are you okay?"
he wants to know, directs me outside for some air. He lets me
tip his eyes with mascara, I've been trying to do it all night.
                          "If it will make you feel better,"
he says, fluttering his lashes and agreeing to lip gloss.
We are in a garden, shrubbery sculpted into dragons and knights.
                          "Get a load of the topiary,"
I say, and he laughs, dances a small pirouette through the bushes
before patting my head and leaving with some German girls,
                          "Auf Wiedersehen, good night,"
they sing, and I think about the German people, a strange bunch,
my ex-boyfriend forever apologizing for his grandfather being a Nazi.
                          "It's a funny fucking world,"
he'd sigh as I held a gun to the side of my head, let it slide into my mouth,
he loved that game. I notice blood on my sleeve and slip through
                          sliding glass
back into the party which is really winding down. Two boys from the band
who just signed to Atlantic sit on their kitchen floor strumming guitars.
                          "Do you know the movie game?"
I ask, and the blonde one is being difficult, he starts singing in French,
so I sit down beside him and ask for translation. He says, "I'm not in the mood."
                          "Too bad, I am,"
I quote and he smiles, likes that I know Truffaut, what does he think,
I'm some amateur? Besides, everyone knows you don't start with the French.
                          "You work up to the French,"
I mutter; it goes on like that for a while, until his playing grows restless
and his eyes slide away. I send the other one for cigarettes and lean in for a close-up,
                          "Here's our chance,"
I say, he's wearing one of those designer cowboy shirts, the pearl buttons snap
right open. For a minute I forget my lines, the scene. He puts his hand around my neck
                          and it's that easy.

Jailhouse Rock

In jail there is some paperwork. The desk clerk takes my name
and information, although I already gave it to the lady police officer

along with my shoelaces. Beside me, the blonde in an orange jumpsuit
is talking about noodles. "They give them to us cold in commissary

because we aren't allowed to have hot water. Now, what do you think of that?
Cold noodles!" I think I prefer them that way, soba, but I don't say it

since I feel like such an asshole for thinking it that a buzzing starts in my ears,
but I can still hear her, see her clearly, and the long line of men who shuffle past

in green polyester. "They look like turtles, don't they." I wish I were a turtle
hunched over like them, heads bowed as though sinking down into their necks.

The last one sings a little song under his breath, it's a song about pussy; "Oh, that pussy divine,
that pussy so fine…" This goes on for a long time, I can hear him humming all night

in the cell next to mine, so although I can't see him, I know he's there, the way
I feel the tire iron still there, clasped in my hand after an ex showed up at the party

with a knife and a song of what he would do–kill me then kill himself, that old classic.
And even though I know he's sick, know I didn't ask for this, still

I asked for something. I can't pretend I don't like a mad dog around
to put down. I'm going to find a way to invite that mad dog in, to give him treats

and kick him just to hear him whine and bark. If I barked all night
in my cell, I'd be back-up for this guy, the end of the line.

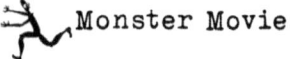

Thigh Gap

(A Golden Shovel after Plath's "Edge")

Our sorority had group showers. The
max was ten, but one Alpha Gam woman

counted only half. When she turned side, the thought—is
Jen going to slide down the drain? I gaped at bones perfected,

straining against skin. Then dinner, water and kale, explained how her
mother said the body needs less than you think, urged against dead

animal flesh hanging around the colon. What else about the body?
Let's see—this was the 1990s, a few years before women's wears

became the shrine of lack, designed explicitly so that the
desired blank space between would be highlighted, a thigh smile.

When my own twin began her mission to evanesce, I thought again of
Jen, and the force of will needed to starve into lessness. Her accomplishment,

harrowing though it was to watch, awed me, undisciplined witness. The
notion that a body could be denied what it asked seemed like magic, an illusion

cast—like a smiling woman in the conjurer's box sawed in half. And of
those spectators sat front row for the winnowing show, myself and sisters a

candlelight ritual and hefty check had anointed—what shall we spin? Pseudo-Greek
women woven tight by summer rush earned the right (in system born of necessity)

to sleep and sup together in red brick manses clung high with ivy. Song flowed
from each lead-paned window, glowing coed girls framed like Juliets, humming in

startling harmony, winsome tunes to lure new recruits and lettered men below. The
need to please, to Siren-call fresh bodies as maidens and escorts, set forth in scrolls

seen only in sacred ceremony. Yet the requisite was daily clear— numbers of
our brood must grow, and boys must find us pleasing here. For Jen, nests of her

white-blonde curls swirling our shared drains, her knife of a body in toga
cinched tight for Kappa Psi keggers, approval was met. We touched her

shoulders lightly with our swords, we traced the soft downy hair furring bare
skin, we offered accolades for cessation of her menses, a blood relief. At her feet,

humble gifts were laid—air-popped corn, gummy worms, Dexatrim. A war, it seemed,
was underway, and we the Athenian fleets. Disloyal, I dreamed of retreat; followed Jen to

the womb-like room where, both red and helpless under hot shower's spray, our be-
ings briefly matched. Go back, I said, Penelope at her loom, forget what the others are saying

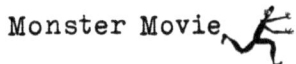

and return to safer shores. Or maybe just stared at protruding ribs until she felt it and said, "We need to beat Tri Delta," which was true. I could barely make out her form through the steam, "I have,"

she said dreamily, "considered my thighs," then grasped my dimpled thighs and squeezed. "Come with us," she said, "reduce." Present day, there is you, listening. You ask if this really happened, so

I say, Panhellenic sage; "What is truth, but myth made new?" Did Odysseus really travel unfathomably far, Medusa revenge herself on men with her stone gaze, Demeter weep at the swallowed seed, it

having hurled her daughter into hell? "All our favorite horror stories," I say. "And your twin?" you ask. "She is still here," I say, "has shed the ancient skin." To self, *she begins*. The world, of course, is over.

Cinema

She got off the bus from Muncie with only the yellow dress she was wearing, ballet flats and a fifty-dollar bill pinned to her bra. There were stars in her hair and ribbons in her eyes. Back home was haunted, but here she was hollow, new. Heat from the street grate blew her hem up, corn cob with the husk stripped clean. Cute meet on 45th, "You need a martini," her him said, and she sipped gin around olives in the Signature Room while he blew in her seashell, nipped down her strap, gave her the slip. *There's more than one way to skin an ape,* she thought later on her park bench, all Midwest grit. Stars yoked the sunrise, wrecked the night. At the diner, ordered Eggs Benedict on a whim with the last of her cash then stared aghast at what she got. "Eggs on eggs," sighed the waitress, "and your check."

Ode to the Bramford, *Rosemary's Baby*

Guy has a swagger that's hard to deny and the neighbors are so friendly. Natives of this brownstone, they ply Ro with vodka blush and chocolate mousse, a mix delivering bad dreams of mouse bites, storms at sea, a pope insisting that she kiss his ring. Some say the Bramford has a bad history—covens, and a man who ate his own baby. Rosemary does not believe, hangs curtains, cleans the oven, feeds Guy tuna sandwiches on white, buys plump pillows for the window seat, ignores the chanting she hears through walls at night, tries to make this place to make this place *I will make a home.*

Election Night Noir: Chicago, 2000

Kate knows the owner so we're in, no cover. It's called RedNoFive, "Like the chemical," says Jimmy, "you know, that dye." I hear die and I'm mystified, more so when Kate screams in my ear, "The club, the club!" Who's dying? Who has a club? Someone hands me a vodka and Red Bull and Jimmy's stripper girlfriend smiles. In the strobe light her white lace shirt seems rosy, like the skin when the window came down on me breaking into my own place, shredded and delicate. "I remembered my keys tonight," I say, and Kate gives me a kiss, "City mouse!" she says. The boy sitting next to me pulls a bag of marshmallows out of his backpack and places it in his lap. "Don't fuck with him, he's Russian," says Jimmy, "no habla inglés." He tugs on my newly blue hair. "I hate it," he says brightly, then takes Kate and his girlfriend whose name no one knows to do a bump or two in the bathroom. Later, we will end up in the hospital when Kate's heart stops, and the doctor will write on his prescription pad, "Quit snorting coke." The boy has started placing marshmallows in his mouth one after the other with no signs of stopping. "That's not something we do here," I say, watching him swallow. He's halfway through the bag with eyes closed, as though someone is giving him the host. I snap fingers in front of his face like he's my dog, then stop, horrified. "What am I doing," I say. "I should go get her." He's tapping his toes to the music, Frankie Knuckles singing *You Can't Hide*. "I saw a ghost this morning," I say, "He looked like Carey Grant." I raise my voice a little and try to harmonize with the song, "I think I'm losing my mind." He opens his eyes and reaches in his bag for the last marshmallow, then sort of shoves it in my mouth. "We don't have these where I come from," he says in clipped, perfect English. "What a country."

Early-Aughts Drama: Hansen's Basement, Wicker Park

1. The Game

Later, I know what you will want, but right now we are playing ping-pong.
If we keep doing coke, I think, *there won't be time for sex,* so I ask for another line.
My paddle is pink, the plastic cover peeling back like a flap of skin, and you
take it from me, press down so the gluey mess beneath is hidden, tap out the powder.

Ceiling pipes steam the cement, and the music so loud it seems to bounce off walls
like the ball between us, coming fast now but I can't seem to miss. I begin
to beat you, and sing along with my shots, "Drop it like it's hot, drop it like it's hot,"
and you start laughing, take off your shirt and wrap it around your head like a soldier.

In that moment, I love you and even say it out loud, "I love you, Andy," and
I'm barely considering the coke in your pocket. "I don't know why
I was so mean to those other guys, but I'm glad I'm not to you. Right?"
You start nodding, I smile and nod too, and then we decide to keep it up,

keep bobbing our heads while the game continues because it's funny, also harder
than I thought, especially when you slam the walls shots and all at once I'm losing,
I put down my paddle, but you're still shaking your head only side to side now, and
when I go to put my hand on your arm, you're shaking all over: you tell me, "Stop."

2. Andy Speaks

When I met her for the first time, I fell off my chair, climbed back on, then fell again—
you know, the gin. It was easy, I just BS'd about those Brontes and Jane Austen. Hell,
I took English 101. She never seemed to notice I was on my sixth, or sixteenth drink,
of course, she had her own, and her smile, that million-dollar grin she had, all innocent.
She smiled, smiled, kept on smiling for two years, everything I did, golden.

Then she turned like a screw, yeah, I read that too, she always thought I was dim, I knew it all along,
knew it even when she didn't know it. What did she know? Where did she think it came from,
the diamonds and the dinners out, leather pants and Amsterdam? I mean *Amsterdam* for Chrissakes,
all that hash and blow and bought and sold; I'm a businessman. Big Six firm by day
the rest just a side, and since when won't sugar melt in her mouth

or up her nose, right? That's one game she pretends not to play, she's busy with her own,
they're called poems. And while she fingerpaints and whines and moans, I'm goddamn Zeus,
I control the weather, only backwards; I open up my umbrella and it snows. That's where
we keep it, me and Hansen, all that coke in the folds, they never look there, and when we sell
sometimes if flows too fast, like that time she rode along, "Just to see," she said.

What she saw was some guy nearly giving me head when the stash got dumped in my lap,
"Shame to waste it," he said and handed me the cash—*sold*. She cried then. But later,
she was fine, even tried it herself for the first time and then it was all she wrote and wrote
and kept on writing and talking, every guy at every party hears her speed freak speech
on Whitman and shit, she thinks they're listening when they're staring at her tits, Christ,
her cornfield-small-town shtick gets old. She's crazy; I honestly think she's crazy,

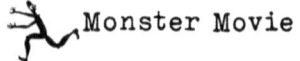

no way she knows how to live in the world, I hold her hand, I help her cross the street,
she's like a child, a helpless child or maybe it's me, I'm crazy, maybe I am, because
she's sweet though and I love her, it's sick how I've loved her, and don't I pay the bills?
Look at her; coked to the gills, shaking while she lights a cigarette, asks Hansen for a Pepsi
and some pills. Skirt riding up, I'll have that later, do whatever I want; I'm so tired of this cunt

telling me about those other guys, and all the while, her smile, that smile, that purr–
When *I* smile, I'm thinking of bombs in her mailbox, cockroaches set loose in her walls…
She can't leave me, she better never leave me. Oh God, I'm sorry, I'm so sorry,
if I could take it back I would, but I can't pour it back in the vial, in the bottle
and tonight, she'll remember who I am—who I am and what I taught her.

Pick-Up Line Triolet with Cocaine: Elbo Room, Chicago

She likes a line now and again, that's all.
"Did it hurt when you fell from heaven?"
he asks, then if she wants to party in the stalls.
She'd like a line now. And again. That's all
it takes to hit the ceiling, star the neon, small
the world beneath. Red-lit faces, cracked shot glass
held at fractured lines again. She likes it all.
How everything hurts when she falls! Heaven.

Alan Solomon's Gold Coast

The lovely reality about the Gold Coast neighborhood, part of the Near North Side community, is that although it is Chicago's wealthiest area and its shops largely cater to Chicago's wealthiest residents, nothing prevents the rest of us from appreciating their good fortune and good taste.
–Alan Solomon, "Explore Chicago"

What is a coast without gold? Coasting through life is easier with gold, lickety-split
that lick-it-up trick when the gold flows liquid on your tongue you've won, it's a rush,
let's rush to Rush Street, window shop at Vuitton, Lanvin, the skin of patrons so taut
they're mannequins, faces creamed with flecks of, specks of, *Sold.*
And the pennies from heaven aren't copper, that talk is derby, fedora, it's just
old hat, fat cats in top hats, is there anything cuter than pets in spats?
Walk along the coast with your golden lab and stroller, baby topped with a tiara
those stones aren't real. No need to be gauche when there is so much to go around,
right? Left? We're Near North and all you need to remember
is which way's the lake to get your bearings in this bullish tide awash the coast
and condos that are coast-ish, coast-adjacent, new high-rises and old brownstones
on Oak, Clark, Lake Shore Drive, those streets are paved with oh, you know.

The End is The Beginning: Music Box Theatre, Chicago, Memento Opening Night

When we try to see it again the next day, stumbling hungover down Southport under a High Noon sun, a sign on the door: *Theatre closed. Rats.*

We stay in our seats, sink down low and hope to catch the midnight screening. The man with a flashlight is polite. Show's over, folks.

House lights come up slowly while sun and clouds move across the ceiling. I can feel Andy breathing beside me. "What just happened?" he says.

It gets bloody, then he starts to fade, to blank. *Can I just let myself forget what you made me do? Will I lie to myself to be happy?*

In the movie, the girl tricks the boy, fakes a black eye, hides all his pens. This happens again and again.

Andy puts his arm around me, spills popcorn down my blouse, fishes it out. "In the suburbs, we won't drink so much. How many babies do you want?"

He's so blonde, it can't be real. She turns him toward the mirror, undresses him slowly to reveal tattoos all over his body, they can't be real.

On screen, the man runs between parked cars, believes he's chasing someone, then gunshots. He's being chased. I laugh until Andy makes me stop.

I have this condition, he says, after trying to pay the motel guy twice. "Short term memory loss," whispers Andy, downs his beer, winks.

The main character sits on a bed in a motel room by himself, considers harm— lightly touches bandages on his thighs, his arms. If there was a woman there before, she's gone

"This is all backwards," says Andy, "or maybe I'm backwards." "I'm forwards," I say. He says, "You're upside down." He's funny, which I like. I decide to remember this, delete how he chooses coke over me.

Cut in. Man holding an instant photo. As he shakes it, the photo blurs, fades to blank. Photo back in the camera, bullet back in the gun, scream back in the mouth.

Inside, an orange sun and feathery clouds are projected across the ceiling. We rest our heads on the seatbacks, stare up until the lights come down.

It's a cool Chicago night as we stroll down Southport, beer bottles in our back pockets. One slips, shatters on the sidewalk. Andy says, "Keep walking."

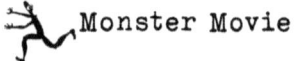

South Side Sonnet

You don't have to say what side of the city
you come from, but you say it anyway. Hell,
you scream it. Gold chain, accent like a bell
that's cracked, blue tee that reads *Union bids*

do it better, hockey gear in the bed of your truck,
faded Comiskey tickets on the dash, the rush
to hold my door for me, Slovak eyes and hushed
country CD with endless Waco Brothers' tracks.

It's overkill, like the building site we drive to
that first night, the brick you laid by hand, red dust
in the air, on our skin, the punch of lime and rusting
trowels: it's my family's farm but harder and I love you

five years for it. Then I cheat, sleep with those I know
you hate—North Shore boys from the right side of Chicago.

Triolet 007: My Biopic

There are always two girls in a Bond flick:
One who will make it, the other who won't.
Deciding which one you are is the trick.
There are always two girls in a bind. Be quick
Because James wants to put out the lights, *click—*
Are you twin sets and sock hops, or safe words and chokes?
There are always two girls. *Tick tock tick.*
One who will make it, the other who won't.

Locusts II. Winter, 2006

I find shed locust skin in the windowpane,
attach it to my sweater like a brooch.
"Do you like my jewelry," I say, turning back
to where you lie in bed. "That's filthy," you reply,

"Come here." You start removing clothes, my top layer
quickly, I can feel the hard insect shell slide
over my cheek. The rest, you take your time.
During sex, a ribbon of menstrual blood and you keep going

for a moment, but your face. Like you've seen
a car accident, limbs separated from bodies in a soggy crunch
of metal. When you give up, slide off me and scramble
to the bathroom, I pull crisp linen to my chin.

Then I throw it off, roll to a ball at the edge of the bed
trying to keep my legs together, aware of how you feel
about your sheets. These *are* nice sheets I think,
my face pressed sideways so that objects seem to float–

nice chair, nice rug… Your cat drifts by, her patchy tail
skimming my skin. You *are* a nice cat? I try it out in my head
even as she fixes me with yellow eyes and mouths a silent growl.
"I'll crucify you, kitty," I whisper, picturing tiny paws nailed

to the headboard, picturing you stretched beside her, skinned.
I can't make it stop. Emerging in a cloud of shower steam,
you wrap me in a towel, pull me onto your lap, say sorry. "It's okay,"
I say, thinking I *am* a nice girl. Thinking, *I'll make you pay.*

Feature

Haunted House II: The Return

1. **Exterior**

Establishing shot: Buick wagon pulls up long gravel drive to farmhouse. Clapboard, the white paint is peeling, gray beneath. Jump cut: cornfields look disordered, sere. Adult twin daughters, one with fried and dyed red hair, wander listlessly between rows. "A single drink from the well, you'll see," their mother says, sun reflecting off glasses, veiling her eyes. "Sweetest water on earth." Close-up: the pump coughs brown then a clear stream flows. Lead role: folding in half at the hip, the crimson twin parts lips and swallows metal, mumbles to no one, "A mouthful of cold pennies." Sideways through the water ribbon she watches her father kneel, crumble dry soil in his hands, then shake head hard as though to unloose a buzzing. Savvy viewers understand the father is compromised.

2. **Interior**

Time skip: post-sunset. The house is dark and still, all glass panes sealed shut. The mother lights candles, rooms choked with old furniture—"There, that was my childhood bed. Your grandfather carved it by hand." Family eats sandwiches packed for the trip and red twin blows out flames. Sisters share the bed. Dream sequence: a cloaked figure moves slowly on the second floor, candle in hand, then down steep staircase to touch fire against drapes, table linens, photographs that curl in the burn, before leaving and barricading the exit. Our lead (who will die first—twist!) struggles awake to see mother standing at the black window. The night seems to gain entry, enfold her like a swarm of black flies. Voiceover: *I thought it would be different this time.* The audience sees that sleep, waking—nowhere is safe. Daughter whispers her mother's name, but she won't answer.

Interregnum

Every morning I mistake my cat's warmth and think
the one who left me has returned to finish the job.
I think about Sunbeam bread and ice rinks.
I think about ledgers and Blue Island.
It makes no sense. I stack up words like wood
for a winter storm, I make soups in bulk
and freeze the Tupperware pots, I buy galoshes
and hot glue guns. I want to be prepared
for whatever comes, I want bars of gold
buried in the yard, I want a tattoo that reads
NUTS TO YOU AND YOUR LITTLE DOG TOO.
I want to know that there's a space across this war
zone where I can lay down my arms and legs
and get a new set of arms and legs that will snap
into place on my count. In my downtime, I intend
to start a garden in the bed of my truck as soon
as I buy my truck, and plant greens and carrots
and begonias around the borders to stave off
rabbits who can't resist carrots, will do anything
to reach carrots, even in soil that's been exhausted.

Ceci n'est pas une pipe

1. This poem is not a poem

It's a request. Could you change the selection on the jukebox? There's a tear in my bear. Beer. The rest is Memorex. How do you get from here to there and back again? Tell me, how do you break the sound barrier? When I was young, I was afraid of bears. Beers. I used to drink them with an orange juice back just to chase it down. The townies would laugh, they requested I return my townie card. No cred. What's a girl got to do around these parts to hear a little music? Be born and bred? If I had some bread, I'd be gone from here. Again. Then I'd return because that's the law of returns; you break it, you buy it, *caveat emptor*, even on the beer you sink. Everything but the kitchen sinking. I could learn to like this place if everyone would just hit erase. From my window, bears.

2. This poem is not a poem

It's a contract. You've already started reading, so you are signed, sealed, arrived on the dotted whatever. How far are you willing to blow? Breathe out. Now. Feel that? That's bubble gum on your face, you tried to impress your friends and just made a mess. That's mud in your stye of an eye if you take my bleeding and you have to, need to. Otherwise, why go on? I can't go on. I'll fucking go on. Godot only knows what's on the menu for this evening, guvnor. Don't order the special. Rookie move, they use brunch steak left over from yesterday for the rest of the week. It's special, you're special, let's all follow our dreams and see where they break us. While you're up, be a dear and ask the girl for the check. She'll say sign here.

3. This poem is not a poem

It's a confession. I shot my woman down. Then I shot her again and the horse she rode in on. Next, I wrote a song about it so every hombre west of the Pecos would know I'm a bad, bad man. That horse's name was Strawberry. I make a mean shortcake but never from scratch. When I have an itch, I do what needs done, and it spreads like jam on bread. Jam and bread! What a song. Austria and Nazis, only true love could get the Von Trapps out of that scrape. The heart is offered and it's red jelly, red tape, scraps. What I kill, I kill dead.

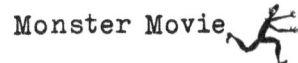

Baby Shower Torture Porn: Rolling Meadows, Illinois

"This is how I'd do it," she says.
Strawberry cake with a buttercream frost and the knife,
when it enters, slides in clean. "Pretend it's his eyeball,"
she says, twists the knife quickly then inserts her fork.
"Delicious," she says, raising a bite to her mouth. "Yes,"
says the hostess, "yes, the berries keep it moist."
"I'd use a screwdriver to the jugular; you have to be fast. Tea?"
she asks me, the only baby-less attendee, pours hot herbal
into my cup. We all have tea in bone china decorated
with daisies, and as the steam rises
my blonde, Kate Spaded couch-mate murmurs,
"Boiling water and a hammer to the skull, no sugar for me, thanks."
"Not that I'd enjoy it," she says, studying my face, "but I would
take a wrench to his knees." "Who?" I ask. "Anyone," she says. "You'll see."
She pats my belly and tells me she keeps a butcher knife
under her pillow, and then the men come in, the husbands
home from work in flat front khakis and collared shirts. They are
shy and cologned and pulling at their ties, but they eat the cake
we press on them; we insist they eat every last slice.

Bad Robot

A boy hates his mom. Something's gone
wrong; wires split and fizzing in an angry brain.
What faulty AI maker is responsible for this one?
No parts work as they should anymore, maintenance

is down and the model is already out of date. Wait—
were they meant to get a new unit? Obsolescence is close
to adolescence—both ask reckoning. Now hang tight
while data scans: "The snow cannot forgive us," he says; goes

on, "An aftermath of traps." And "You're a bitch, mom," that classic.
The metal was meant to protect, encase, but maybe flesh
is preferable. In the night, he wakes with fever flashing
and stumbles to her room, allows her touch. She has wished

for this—gently brushing back his damp hair—even when
he said he dreamed her dead. Everything here a weapon.

Ode to the Rain, *Three Days of the Condor*

Redford's Turner takes the back way when it rains, and he's on the hook
for office lunch. Hunched under tweed, he runs alleys behind the
American Literary Historical Society at Park and Lex where he is an archivist, except
it is not the American Literary Historical Society and Turner is not an archivist.
Driving rain, and the spate hides Turner from the watching man who will invade
while Turner buys sandwiches for his colleagues, with his gun will lay waste.
A storm falls differently in a city than anywhere else, the way no two bodies
fall the same. When Turner returns from the luncheonette, it's all over
and he calls it in to the Agency where they ask for details: death count, bullet caliber,

his code name, but Turner can't conjure Condor. *I don't remember yesterday. Today it rained.*

Fat Tuesday in New Orleans, 2009

Eddy makes us climb up on the roof.
It's really high and I think, *I'm 33, when
do I stop climbing on the roof?* I can't believe the city
how perfect, like a doll's town   A view
to the river
Katrina's X-painted houses too far to see

Then we're sitting on the front stoop of their shotgun house
whiskey and coffee
Tori talks of beignets in the French Quarter but right now
Eddy is playing his guitar
in the sunshine

It's so warm
I take off my shoes and socks and their cat Mohammad
stretches out on my toes

Tori has a smudge of pink paint left on her face

Next door neighbors stop by   circle on the sidewalk
Girl wearing a crown and mismatched socks
one purple one red
Boy with tiger stripes smeared across his cheeks
holding a banjo   and another boy, wild-eyed
who hasn't yet been to sleep

Eddy admires his own gold spray-painted shoes
plays a song he wrote—   *What I owe to Iowa*
He's from Minnesota
Tori asks me about Chicago
and I ask her about Maine

We are all from somewhere   one boy
even from a place called Paradise

Monster Movie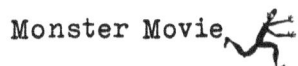

Short Film

June. Drinking beer at the Bluebird Bar which has the distinction of straddling a property line between the richest and poorest counties in Northern Michigan. The room is filthy hot and packed, and I don't fit in; not with the Cedar townie cherry pickers and third-generation fishermen, nor the Leland privileged in their frankly cliché pastel plaids and boat shoes. What I do is keep my head down, drink my Labatt's Blue and try not to flinch when a girl whose beauty guarantees her entry on either side crosses the room from money to minus. The man she walks away from is not happy, and as she takes Jim Burke's hand (he ties my lake trout order with a bow every Friday at the docks) the man whispers, "White trash." There's a moment suspended like a drop of mercury in a thermometer, and I think two things: how unnervingly White every room has been since I arrived and how high the temperature seems to be rising; and then the first glass smashes and the place goes up in flames.

Corsage
after Raymond Carver

You sidle up, a nervous suitor at a dance. Sideways glances at others who are doing it better, crisp black ties, polish on their shoes, the right moves. What kind of dance is this? Your pants are too tight, you're fumbling, all the pretty girls glide away. *The damp fields asleep in moonlight,* you say. The girl's dresses rustle like wheat. Also, *A light wind, and beyond the window trees swimming in the golden morning air.* The chaperone places a heavy hand on your shoulder. "That's no way to speak to a lady," he says. "Maybe you don't belong at this dance." The girls gather whispering against the wall, spring flowers in their pastel frocks. "Absolutely not," says the chaperone, "let me show you the exit." You both turn towards the open window. The stars seem impossibly close. "How many flights?" you ask. The chaperone pats your arm, gives you a gentle shove. "Yes, that's the right question."

Actionville

So much corn dust
choking the air,

watch for deer at night
from fields to blacktop.

Local lore says Underground Railroad
blew through years back—

Asa Talcott's barn
in the part of town called Africa.

We have a bent way of saying
Jacksonville now,

now the barns and sheds
burn hot meth and scent sweet ether.

Dreams of home chase me down
in dark, so that my sleep-self picks

drowning over fire: a rain-swollen creek
that rises to swallow crops, homes, squeals

of hogs in pens, men in Morgan County prison

and the Ferris wheel invented here,
once the highest drop in town.

All-American Extraterrestrial

All my life I've lived between the lines
of tilled fields, luxuriated in order

created by man and machine. The land
is owned here and known, so when a patch

grows wild, we lay blame. There is safety
in deeds, in bills of sale signed plainly, even if

most landlords here are absentee. What I see
every evening on my drive home from work is green,

mile after mile: swaying soybean leaves, barley shocks
tall stalks of ripening corn. Farm boy rhymes

with Illinois, and these fields are lousy
with them in summer. They are beautiful, too,

because what I'm talking about is a certain flavor of it,
beauty—the boys shirtless on tractors in late June sun

side-dressing nitrogen and crop scouting rows. The blight
now is how strange everything seems since space men came

in the night to take me off-planet, deposited me sleeping
in a house that looks like my house, in a town very like

my small town, a place familiar, I've been in this state before,
this country, I'm sure of it, but no. You've all changed faces.

Movie Soundtrack: Tom Petty's "American Girl"

You have to take it easy, baby, and make it last all night
to be a real American girl. To be a real boy, everyone knows
takes bravado and no more nose-growing, Pinocchio. Lighten
up, take it easy, don't be a baby, baby. Gender is fluid all night,
you could be anyone under the stars. Stripes, spots, let's get this right—
girls will be boys and boys will kill girls. We count the rows.
Baby, you'll take it. It's easy. We make it all feel like night.
Girl? Boy? Everyone knows America isn't real.

Period Piece

Not the hunting scene for Swiss-made clocks, they prefer chalet
with waterwheels, beehives, dancing milkmaid figurines. German style, though,

goes totally Black Forest. Think hand-carved horn and rifle intertwined, think
stag and rabbit hanging from a cabin wrapped with vines. The hunter slides out

to sing his beer-drinking tune *Ein Prosit,* then back around to hide. Which will you choose,
cuckoo lover? Does it help to know components? German clocks are German all through,

while in Zurich, two parts are paired. The wooden roof caps a brass heart, mechanical piece shuttered deep, alien. What I'm saying—Suisse and Deutschland share the same insides.

All clock movements are made in Bavaria, inner workings so specialized that the practical
Swiss lost interest. What *they* create will always be needed—painted skin of Lindenwood

to shelter metal guts and then the bird itself, guaranteed to spring and sing on the hour
when wound. The Swiss have always appreciated cover, chocolate and watches stretched

across an entire country rigged with explosives buried far and set to blow. I should know, being
half myself, with a great-grandfather who once ran the place. Family lore states Rudi Minger

granted Hitler's wish to glide his planes far above the Alps, stipulating only that ground entry
must be closed. Strange that the bargain was kept, no black-coated soldiers wandering over

to try and spy Heidi. It goes to show how important the surface—handshake deal, decorative
etching, gloves. Who wants to see the messy underneath, arteries inside the throat? The squeeze.

If still undecided, let me (a completely objective seller) suggest running your hands
across different carvings to feel the rough or gloss, then perhaps slipping fingers into several

clocks. Once you know the system intimately, you understand how it starts and stops.

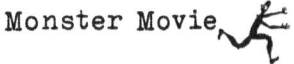

Body Horror: Biopsy

I step through a glass door to the grassy courtyard
outside the clinic waiting room. The sun shines medium.

On the ground, an iridescent grackle faces away,
and I move closer and closer. If I were a hunter, the kill

shot would be easy. She must see something against
the far brick wall that pins her attention, maybe

the bent tree limbs' shadow swaying in the window.
I know I've only been this close to a wild bird

once before when, during census, we caught all
we could in a mammoth net and banded them

before setting free to flight. I held one then, head
pinned between index and middle finger. She

stayed so still, I thought dead for sure. But the leader said
they do that instinctively, go limp in human hands.

When we released all at once, hundreds smeared the clouds
like dark ink on white sheets in a language unfamiliar. This

bird is the distance from you to me. I reach down to stroke glistening
wings and as she turns, I see the hollow where her eye should be.

Ode to the Barn Raising Scene, Peter Weir's Witness

Greater than Rachel making eyes at John Book
over pitchers of cold buttermilk, greater than berry pies
that stretch endlessly over pine tables nestled
in a field of waving green Pennsylvania tall grass, greater even
than a joyful hymn the men sing in communion of their work
while small Samuel Lapp with a small hammer mimics his elders,
is Daniel the Forgotten—clambering up the just built beams
against a backdrop of clear lavender sky, climbing higher
and higher, so sure those boards will hold him.

In a Capsule of the Tanning Salon

The premonition of these UVs on my skin:
Tissue in a bomb-blast wind.

John Hughes Redux

The sudden violence of men is always surprising.
In high school, I walked out after Spanish

smiling at Rich. He smiled back, reached for my hand,
but I had forgotten my flute for afternoon band, backtracked

to our classroom to chat with Señora Denny and collect my case.
By the time I caught up with Rich in the hall, he had Russell Poe

in an alcove, beating in his face. Two minutes. It was not
more than two minutes between leave taking and return.

We went to the Christmas Dance because he was beautiful
and I wanted to know the secret to his rage. I burned myself

raw at the tanning salon, wore a blue velvet gown, pierced
my ears with cubic zirconia, followed him home

and into his bedroom, turned the lights low. He never told.

Slapstick: Ear Re-Piercing with Attendant Lexi at Claire's Boutique

When she puts her gun to my head, it feels like any other day—
one more small horror where I'm asked to go along.

"Lexi never misses," she brags, Sharpie marker used to mark the spot
lightly spinning across her fingers like a doll's baton.

It's quick, and she exclaims in wonder, "You didn't flinch!"
I say I can't believe anyone flinches anymore. "Oh,

they're always surprised," she replies. "Isn't that funny?" When she
brushes back my hair, it feels near tender, although the mirror

held up shows reddening flesh around a cheap brass stud. "Raw
for a few days," she murmurs, which seems fair. I hand her cash

and receive a large bottle of soothing solution in return. "That's
Benzalkonium Chloride," Lexi says. "Don't drink it." She winks, mimes

sipping the liquid, then shoos me softly off as I try to extend
our moment, ask what else the solution might fix. "They've got

pills for everything," she says, turns grinning to her next patron
as I exit through rainbow scrunchies and unicorn bracelets.

At work the morning before, my officemate handed me a pink heart
sticker emblazoned in glitter letters; YOU ARE SPECIAL, suggested new

jewelry to lift my spirits. "Let's smile," she said, "every day above ground is a gift."
She told me two true tales of child death, one so brutal I went to a panic

room in my mind, the other ending with a carved granite bicycle statue on
a headstone. She said, "Don't you find that beautiful? He loved that bike." Then,

"He was so small; the driver never even saw him." What I find is this place unsound.
I wish to forget it all, let the piercing gun go brain-deep and remove children,

gold-plated gems, black markers and blue dots spinning; I requested this wound.

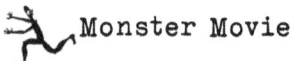 Monster Movie

Tech Enters the Midwest

It slides through the high wires
lacing telephone poles that line
and order the corn fields, teleports

like a redshirt into alien homes,
floral sofas and enormous Curtis Mathes
consoles. It cooks in the screens. Inside

middle management and millennial mouths
tech speaks growth hacks, disruption, and clouds.

There's tech by Xbox, by blood thinner, by Android.
Tech by bits and bytes, mods and runs.

Tech comes to Titus in his blue room.
At twelve, tech hums past Thor posters,
past penguin pillow pals and Minecraft Steve.

He is held fast by headphones and flickering images cast
from light through the window behind him, fires
burning from every home as evening comes.

Choose-Your-Own-Adventure

All I write about is terror lately, but that's only because
I'm terrified. Just now, while in the bathroom, I heard the doorbell ring
and thought two things: *Can't a girl get a minute?* and *Now where
did I put that machete...* Of course, I don't really have a machete. What
I have is a baseball bat and three full sets of kitchen knives stockpiled
in my world-traveler days (Mississippi and Michigan). Simpler times! Time
before chokers and high-waisted flares imposed themselves again. We were
so innocent then; our necks bare, our jeans low. How could we know
what awaited; the beauty of our weapons, the question of what they hit. If
you answer the door in pajamas, it will always be a Jehovah's Witness
with a pamphlet inviting you to *Peace, Health, Prosperity—Everyone's Dream!*
If you ignore the door and screen your phone, there will be a message from
your mother-in-law to say her dog is dead. If you want, you can go back to bed.

Charley Horse

While you sleep, decisions are made. Your body,
so long on your side, casually switches allegiances

and seizes territory, like a guest suddenly lunging
across the dinner table at their host. If this were war,

and it is, you just lost. Aerial view, a drone might survey
the damage: rough terrain, expanse of sweaty limbs surprised

into agonized spasm, eyes squeezed shut. You're dreaming, sure,
but the pain is real, the way they say a patient feels everything

on the operating table, then forgets. This is night. In day, thoughts
and bones remain your own, right? You're awake, it only feels

like dream, like starring in your own surreal show. Take this scene— that's you
teaching first week of class, mind blown at the faces. Keen and raw like baby birds

who wait on your worm words, they yawn covertly under bangs and baseball caps, smile
shyly at their feet. Late teens, all are beautiful; shiny, a little zitty, seemingly unconcerned

with the grammar test that's next. One student breathes the periodic table
for another course, her mouth forming Hydrogen, Nitrogen, Noble Gas.

Two boys softly toss a hacky sack back and forth between their rows, ignore
minor glowering from those in the seams. Crosscurrents do not bother most,

head-phoned and Apple-Androided as they are, and then the bell sounds and you
announce the day's vocabulary word; "Lade," you say, which makes them laugh even

when you clarify, "Past form of laden: to put a load or burden on." Something goes wrong then,
they stop paying attention because a bell is ringing again but shriller, more insistent and

from everywhere at once. When you freeze, they are kinder than they need to be.
"This must be your first," one says, gets up to close and lock the door

while the others, in pairs and silent, turn heavy tables over.

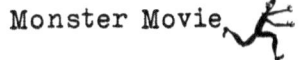

Rated R: Dumb Bitch

"Tattooed on the inside of her lip," my friend's daughter Anna says, peeling back her mouth to demonstrate
where her college roommate inked the message in black block caps. "It's her party trick," she says, bares

perfect teeth while pressing her own bottom lip obscenely against her chin, then waggling wet skin
in my direction. I say it must be a feminist joke, and Anna shakes her head, "I don't think she cares

about any of that." Next, I guess a performance piece, art carved on the body yet hidden within,
shared only with those in the know. Anna says no. "You think too much," she says, which is true, I do think

to the point of pain, my brain sizzling inside its skull like thoughts shocked by a faulty wall socket.
If the tattoo were mine, it would signify the times I didn't leave when I still could, the men

I did not stop hard enough, my scream a whisper, my fists a joke. Those needled words would choke
any plot twist I think I'm owed, so I would know when the knife comes down in my horror story,

I'm not rising again in the last act. No, that's my final scene, gutted and gasping, the interminable girl
who doesn't know she's dead yet and decides to crawl through the mud to the edge of the woods,

the audience yelling to watch out, "He's behind you," and this time he's come back with an axe…
That hands-and-knees creep is the best part, feeble Hail Mary that makes everyone cheer the dumb bitch

slaughter. "I'm glad I never had a daughter," I tell Anna, who laughs and says not to get worked up.
"Everything's fine," she says, "See?" And she shows me a waterfall of roommate photos on her phone,

cascading shots of sunny hikes, blue lake splashes, hugs with puppies, and a valedictorian speech.
In each, you can just see the shadow on her lip, and Anna touches screen—"it means nothing, nothing."

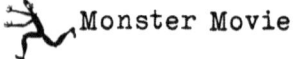

Graffiti Rondeau

"Be cool, girls" scrawled on the unisex bathroom stall
of this hipster dive bar—so legit, Pabst is all
they have on tap. Stark in black marker, a plump peach
emoji and disembodied cock make a teach-
      able moment for patrons, squat waiting last call.

And will you heed the graffiti's plaintive cry, tall
and slightly whiny the order? Laugh, but this wall's
words and symbols speak primal truth, slim may the reach
      be. Cool girls

know the art adjacent matters too—such a small
skull and crossbones, such a tiny Glock drawn… A ball
in miniature clearly had, day at the beach
for the tagger sketching his (of course *his*) dream preach—
take the hint and the eggplant or we'll morgue you, you'll
      be cool girls.

Ode to "Sikiliza Kwa Wahenga," *Get Out*

The film opens on a leafy, well-lit street identical to any in a prosperous suburb or gated community (read: White fear). On his cell phone and out of place, Logan King is lost. He talks to someone on the other end, asks directions and bemoans being late for his jazz gig. When a car draws up alongside and parks, motor running and stereo trilling "Run Rabbit Run," Logan doesn't need to be told twice. "Not today," he mutters, crossing the cobblestones and walking fast in the opposite. This will not save him. The reprieve would be to exit this horror movie, to exit this horror country, seek safety in a place less obsessed with melanin and hate, who knows? Maybe outer space. We can't see who delivers the blow, just dragging feet and the trunk shut tight. Jump cut. Tall pines blur by and the sound of a stringed instrument plucked rough and glum, then whispers in Swahili in minor key, loosely translated and too late for Logan—*Listen to your ancestors. Something bad is coming.*

Rerun

In *My So-Called Life,* the character of Tino
is always off-screen. For the one season

run you never see him, but everyone knows
he's the coolest and feels his absence keenly.

Charismatic lead singer of Frozen Embryos
who quits the band for reasons unknown, Tino

grows larger in our minds the longer we are
denied him, a Minotaur roaming cold corridors

to conjure all that might have been. When Tino
is mentioned the viewer can't help but run film back;

recall the time on a train speeding across Scotland
when a beautiful boy sat down opposite, smiled

at my Chicago ball cap and asked me about America.
"Stop off for a while in Glasgow," he said after hours of chat.

"Let's continue this." Remiss! I pushed on to Edinburgh, late
for another dreary castle tour, then did the same in Seattle

when a tall, gray-eyed man by the jukebox took my hand
and asked me to choose a song. I chose wrong, left with friends

(not wanting to trouble) and assuming there would be more.
Now I know the truth—abundance is for the young. Night

brings dreams to play out my unseen storylines: exes who
love me again (bad deeds forgiven), Ph.D. completed and red

clay soil of Mississippi not so haunting, Brent well and whole
arteries unblocked and back to following Phish, I wish

to follow the plot where my neighbor's dog gets walked
instead of whimpering in a shit-filled backyard behind fences,

or the one where my twin and I live by the blue, blue sea.
Drop the string that leads you back, Tino says. *Stay here with me.*

We've Hardly Begun And

already have ruined this great
bullish experiment, the shining hill
city with no real sense of lasting
design or weight, flowers placed on an
empty casket. Too late. Most mistake any men in scrubs
for doctors: dazed by the prospect of good health, patients
guess incorrectly. Then, when begins the pitch—
"Hey! A medical supplies salesman? Who let you
in the operating room?" It is flim-flam for sure, like no
jam on your peanut butter sandwich, or the
knife used to slice strawberries from the garden twitching
loose to nick your thumb. You should be careful,
maybe look for helpers in the world, those
nice morticians coming from upstate to move bodies
out of overcrowded NYC. See? It's not hard to
plan ahead, to make wishes known so you don't end up
queued last and lonely, hoping for a
real doctor or sandwich maker, at the very least
some daisies to brighten this empty room. That may be
too big an ask: butter yellow when the skies grow gray and we are
under it all—sleet and hail, gale-force winds, snakes leaking
venom as they fall from above and land to wrap around our
wrists like bracelets, like something gold and rubied
Xena might wear when she arrives to save our skin. "I'll always be with
you," she says, right after accidentally stabbing her best friend.
Zoinks! Bet you didn't see that coming—the end, I mean. The end.

Ode to Lynyrd Skynyrd, "Tuesday's Gone"

Over grapefruit beers I say to my husband T, what a shame that certain songs have been taken from us by being overplayed. I'm pissed we missed out on "Free Bird," a lush tune now ruined; those radio DJ's spinning the disc over and over until all meaning fled. But think of Jenny in *Forrest Gump,* I say, a kind of movie version of this rule—too much, I know! That goddamn box of chocolates on every channel, and yet there is that scene—Jenny teetering on the balcony's edge, a gold lamé bird about to be free… I weep a little and whisper, she transforms into winged mystery. T sighs at my tipsy poetry. For me, he says, coked-up Jenny doesn't save Skynyrd's weak lyrics. We get it. You can't change. Personally, I like weekdays and trains in my songs. Remember "Tuesday's Gone"? *I don't know where I'm going. I just want to be left alone. Well, when this train ends, I'll try again.* Fuck, are you going to leave me? T sips his beer, lands me a kiss. I will if we keep talking about Skynyrd.

Monster Movie

We're headed downstate and Natalie's driving, she insisted, a Chicago girl who's driven across Paris, Tokyo, the left side of London streets like a pro so she can handle *this,* and I wake from a doze to find us weaving on my country road, corn high on either side and Natalie gabbling to herself, "It's so quiet and there's no light but moon and nothing's moving and who knows? Who knows what's going to come across the road, maybe a cow, a cow in the road and what's in those fields, could be a zombie with a machete, I can't see for shit!" And she blows the horn just to have some noise, then I start speaking softly to her like I would a skittish colt while I'm thinking of the girl they found in the fields right around here when I was young and what had been done to her, the condition of the body… Her sister who married a close family friend soon after, that sister's eyes at the wedding, dead. How he took her away to Texas that night, how the marriage was threshed when she came back years later like she couldn't help herself; left husband, children, got in her car one day to go to work and just kept going until she hit Cairo, Illinois, where she stopped, bought a soda pop at Lefty's and decided to climb back inside a curse. Then I think of my own sister for a minute, my twin, but only for a minute because it's all I can stand, like hands around my throat to imagine, how I would howl forever at the rustling of the stalks. That pain feels like it belongs here— prairie madness, accidents with tractors, girls dragged into fields on nights just like this and I'm still talking to Natalie who's calmed some, I tell her we're five miles out at most and she flinches at a coyote's cry; "Werewolves," she whispers, "Ghosts and goblins, I think this place is haunted," and I lie, Midwest stoic—"There's no ghosts."

CREDITS

Hate Watch

"Worst yet," my twin says, finger-punching
the volume button in staccato

like an emaciated lab rat eschewing food
for more cocaine. "This show blows,"

she observes clinically as we sit suspended
in television's green glow, real light

waning outside the window. "Look at this
dipshit," she says, and a rinse of joy

cascades over me like a wave of UV rays, so
metastatically pleased to see the figures on screen

make glossy suburban messes—chubby husband
drunk and spilling mustard down his shirt front,

forgotten hot dogs on the grill starting to sizzle and send sparks
upward, so that swaying leaves on backyard trees catch flame

and his slim blonde mommy-wife clad in white linen arrives
just in time to save the house from fire, the sleeping children

from smoke inhalation and crisped corpse body bags. She is capable
and brave, a technician coaxing him to run through domestic chutes

for Bud Light bribes, dry humps and exasperated grins. Everyone
wins! The husband's blunders make meaning, a blueprint of pure fun

to be studied by my sister and me, mid-life women on a microsuede couch,
who crouch dissecting pratfalls for data, field notes that will lead us to the cure.

"He complains about her to his buddy and eyerolls," my sister says. "Then the episode ends."
They high-five gleefully on screen as do we, tipsy from sipping chardonnay

every time the husband utters man cave, power tools, ball and chain.
It's a binge and without pause the next episode begins

as Titus, my young stepson, enters the living room and catches
the remote I toss, wriggles down between us to watch.

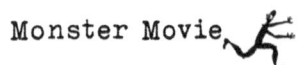

POST-CREDITS

WHO GIVES A RAT'S ASS ABOUT A POEM'S FAITHFULNESS?

Faithful

A famous writer tells me
my poems aren't faithful

She quotes Browning, Rilke,
shuffles pages—see? How hollow

my lines, how trifling they read
when laid like entrails, end to end.

She means to help, maybe. There is
talk of God. What she gets right

are my words' junk hearts. Forget
faith. What good to gossip God now?

He's left the building, no blue
suede shoes for ages and my poems

need to grind. They scorn
one at a time. Yes, my poems

are a little slutty—any partner will do—
all true. What she got wrong

is the tune. It was never Elvis, that
skin suit wrapped around peanut butter

bacon white bread slop. Agreeable to fall
on your knees for pale Jesus in sequins,

a pop hit cobbled of shop-lifted parts—
American Muzak hymns never stop. My

song is less adoptable—a raw cut, a lost
track. My song is a red preemie squalling

and doesn't give a rat's ass about faithfulness.

www.ingramcontent.com/pod-product-compliance
Lightning Source LLC
Chambersburg PA
CBHW041311110526
44590CB00033B/4170